This book belongs to

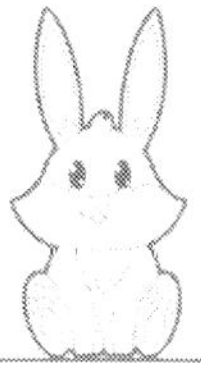

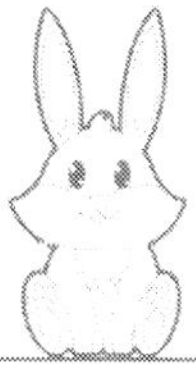

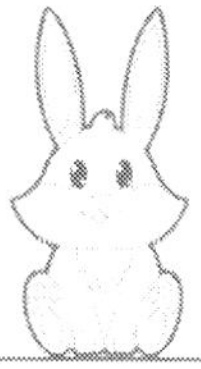

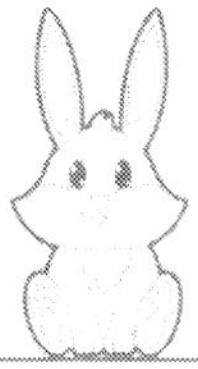

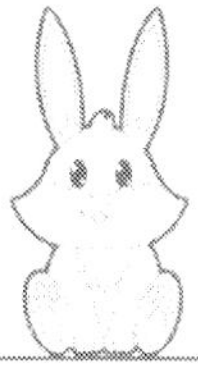

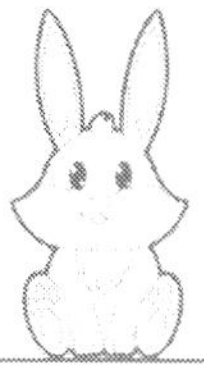

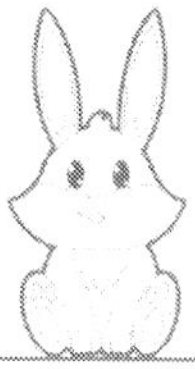

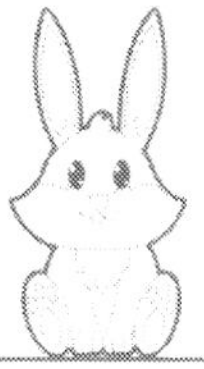

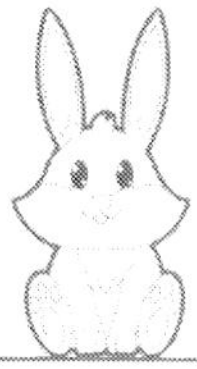

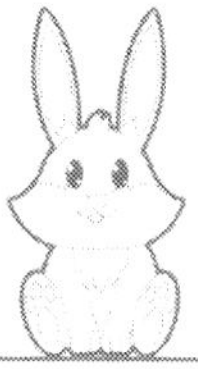

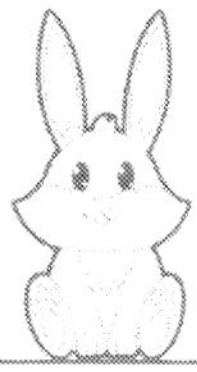

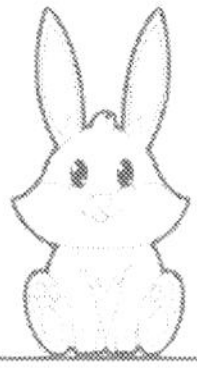

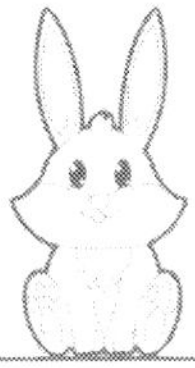

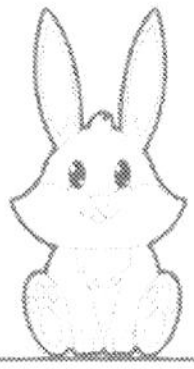

Printed in Great Britain
by Amazon

70885417R00066